Histrionic Persona

Understanding and Conquering Histrionic Personality Disorder

Dr. Emily Stanton

Copyright©2023 **Dr. Emily Stanton**.

All Rights Reserved. No part of this publication may be reproduced or transmitted, in any form or by any means without permission.

Contents

CHAPTER 1 1

Chapter One 1

Introduction to Histrionic Personality Disorder 1

Defining Histrionic Personality Disorder (HPD 1

Historical Perspectives and the Evolution of Understanding 2

The diagnostic criteria and classification 5

Speech is excessively impressionistic and lacking in detail. 6

Prevalence and Demographics 8

Chapter Two 10

Psychological Mechanisms at Play 10

Emotional Instability and Shifting Identity 11

Early life influences and developmental factors 12

Neurobiological Considerations 16

Co-occurring conditions and comorbidities 18

Chapter Three 21

  Case Study 1: Overcoming Social Challenges 21

    Case Study: Overcoming Social Challenges in Histrionic Personality Disorder (HPD) 21

    Case Study 2: Transformative Therapeutic Journeys 26

    Case Study 3: Building Resilience in Everyday Life 32

Chapter Four 40

  Understanding Relationship Dynamics with HPD 40

  Communication Strategies for Partners and Loved Ones 45

  Supporting Friends and Family: A Guide 52

  Professional Perspectives on Relationship Building 56

Chapter Five 69

  Therapeutic Approaches and Interventions for Histrionic Personality Disorder (HPD) 69

Cognitive-Behavioral Therapy (CBT): 69

Cognitive-Behavioral Techniques for Self-Reflection 73

Building a Supportive Network 77

Cultivating Resilience and Shaping a Positive Future Outlook 81

Build Emotional Regulation Skills 83

Chapter One

Introduction to Histrionic Personality Disorder
Defining Histrionic Personality Disorder (HPD)

Histrionic Personality Disorder (HPD) is a psychological condition characterized by a pervasive pattern of excessive emotionality, attention-seeking, and a need for approval. Individuals with HPD often display flamboyant and dramatic behaviors, seeking to be the center of attention in various social situations. They are susceptible to outside influences and have quickly shifting emotions. Relationships with people with histrionic personality disorder can be challenging due to the intense need for reassurance and a tendency to perceive relationships as more intimate than they actually are.

Individuals with histrionic personality disorder often exhibit a high degree of suggestibility, making them susceptible to the influence of others. Their self-expression is often theatrical, and they may use physical appearance to draw attention. Despite their outwardly confident demeanor, there is often an underlying sense of discomfort when not in the spotlight. Moreover, those with HPD may struggle with maintaining deep, meaningful relationships, as their interactions tend to be characterized by superficial charm and a tendency to rapidly shift emotional tones. While they may initially captivate others with their enthusiasm, sustaining these connections can be challenging due to the constant need for affirmation and the potential for emotional intensity.

It's important to note that individuals with histrionic personality disorder may not necessarily recognize the impact of their behavior on others, and the condition can cause distress both for the individual and those around them. Treatment often involves psychotherapy, focusing on developing healthier coping mechanisms, improving interpersonal skills, and fostering a more balanced sense of self.

Historical Perspectives and the Evolution of Understanding

The historical perspective on histrionic personality disorder (HPD) has evolved significantly over time. Initially, traits associated with what we now recognize as HPD were observed and discussed in the early 20th century, but the formal diagnostic criteria and classification emerged later.

Early Observations: Early psychological thinkers, such as Sigmund Freud, touched upon personality characteristics that bear resemblance to aspects of HPD. However, it wasn't until the latter half of the 20th century that these traits were systematically studied.

Inclusion in Diagnostic Manuals: The formal recognition of histrionic personality disorder came with its inclusion in psychiatric diagnostic manuals. The Diagnostic and Statistical Manual of Mental Disorders (DSM) and the International Classification of Diseases (ICD) have outlined specific criteria for diagnosing HPD, providing a standardized framework for clinicians.

Shifts in Understanding: Over time, there has been a shift from viewing personality disorders as static traits to recognizing their potential for change and adaptation. This evolution in understanding has influenced therapeutic approaches, moving towards interventions that aim at improving overall functioning and well-being.

Intersection with Culture: Cultural perspectives have also played a role in shaping the understanding of HPD. What might be considered attention-seeking or dramatic in one cultural context may be perceived differently in another, influencing both diagnosis and treatment considerations.

Psychodynamic Perspectives: Early on, psychodynamic theories suggested that histrionic personality disorder might stem from unresolved conflicts during childhood, particularly in the parent-child relationship. Emphasis was placed on the role of early experiences in shaping the individual's need for attention and approval.

Cognitive and Behavioral Insights: More recent perspectives incorporate cognitive and behavioral elements, emphasizing the role of learned behaviors and maladaptive thought patterns. Cognitive-behavioral therapies have emerged as effective tools for addressing specific behaviors associated with HPD and promoting healthier patterns of thinking and interacting.

Neurobiological Considerations: Advances in neuroscience have sparked interest in understanding the neurobiological underpinnings of personality disorders, including HPD. Research explores how neural pathways, neurotransmitter systems, and genetic factors may contribute to the expression of histrionic traits.

Cultural and Social Influences: The evolving understanding of HPD also acknowledges the impact of cultural and societal norms on the expression and interpretation of certain behaviors. Societal expectations and cultural contexts play a crucial role in shaping how histrionic traits are perceived and assessed.

The diagnostic criteria and classification

The diagnostic criteria and classification of histrionic personality disorder (HPD) provide a structured framework for mental health professionals to identify and characterize this particular personality disorder. These criteria are outlined in widely used diagnostic manuals such as the Diagnostic and Statistical Manual of Mental Disorders (DSM) and the International Classification of Diseases (ICD).

Individuals with HPD often go to great lengths to ensure that they are noticed and may feel uneasy or distressed when not receiving the attention they seek. Interaction with others is often characterized by inappropriate sexually seductive or provocative behavior.

This criterion reflects the tendency of individuals with HPD to use their physical appearance or behavior to draw attention, often in a manner that may be deemed socially inappropriate displays rapidly shifting and shallow expression of emotions; emotions are often exaggerated and may change quickly, contributing to a theatrical and dramatic interpersonal style; consistently uses physical appearance to draw attention to oneself; individuals with HPD may place a strong emphasis on their physical appearance and use it as a tool to captivate others.

Speech is excessively impressionistic and lacking in detail.
The way individuals with HPD communicate may be characterized by a focus on style over substance, with an emphasis on making an impression rather than conveying detailed information

The classification of histrionic personality disorder within the DSM-5 and ICD underscores the importance of recognizing and addressing these patterns of behavior and cognition. The criteria provide a standardized foundation for clinicians to diagnose and differentiate histrionic personality disorder from other mental health conditions, allowing for more targeted and effective treatment strategies.

Beyond the diagnostic criteria, the classification of histrionic personality disorder within the broader landscape of personality disorders emphasizes several key points:

Differentiation from Other Personality Disorders:

While histrionic personality disorder shares some features with other personality disorders, such as borderline personality disorder or narcissistic personality disorder, the diagnostic criteria help clinicians differentiate it based on the specific patterns of attention-seeking, emotional expression, and interpersonal style.

Impact on Functioning:

The classification recognizes that the behaviors associated with histrionic personality disorder can significantly impact an individual's functioning in various areas of life. Relationships, work, and overall well-being may be affected by the need for constant attention and the challenges of forming stable connections.

Developmental Considerations:

The classification acknowledges that these patterns of behavior often emerge early in adulthood and can be enduring. However, it is essential to consider developmental factors and how these patterns may evolve or manifest differently over the course of an individual's life.

Comorbidity and Overlapping Symptoms:

Individuals with histrionic personality disorder may experience comorbid conditions, such as mood disorders or anxiety disorders. The classification recognizes the potential for overlapping symptoms and the importance of addressing the broader clinical picture for comprehensive treatment planning.

Treatment Implications:

The inclusion of histrionic personality disorder in diagnostic manuals directs attention to the need for tailored and evidence-based interventions. Psychotherapeutic approaches, particularly those emphasizing interpersonal skills, cognitive restructuring, and emotion regulation, are often central to the treatment plan.

Cultural Sensitivity:

The classification considers the influence of cultural factors on the expression and interpretation of histrionic traits. This highlights the importance of a culturally sensitive approach to understanding and addressing the disorder.

Prevalence and Demographics

The prevalence and demographics of histrionic personality disorder (HPD) provide insights into the scope of this condition and the populations it affects.

Prevalence:

Estimates of the prevalence of HPD vary, but it is generally considered to be relatively low compared to some other personality disorders. It's important to note that individuals with HPD may not always seek treatment, which can contribute to challenges in determining accurate prevalence rates.

Gender Distribution:

HPD is often diagnosed more frequently in women than in men. The gender distribution suggests that women may be more likely to exhibit the attention-seeking and emotionally expressive behaviors characteristic of HPD.

Age of Onset:

Histrionic personality disorder typically manifests in late adolescence or early adulthood. The attention-seeking and dramatic behaviors associated with HPD may become more apparent as individuals navigate social and interpersonal challenges during this developmental stage.

Comorbidity:

Individuals with HPD may also experience comorbid conditions, such as mood disorders, anxiety disorders, or substance use disorders. The co-occurrence of these conditions can complicate diagnosis and treatment.

Cultural and social influences:

Cultural and societal norms play a role in shaping the expression and interpretation of histrionic traits. The prevalence of certain behaviors associated with HPD may vary across different cultural contexts.

Impact on Functioning:

Histrionic personality disorder can impact various aspects of an individual's life, including relationships, work, and overall well-being. The attention-seeking and emotionally charged interpersonal style may contribute to challenges in forming and maintaining stable connections.

Chapter Two

Psychological Mechanisms at Play

The psychological mechanisms at play in Histrionic Personality Disorder (HPD) provide insight into the underlying processes that contribute to the development and expression of this condition.

Unconscious Desire for Attention and Approval:

Individuals with HPD often have an unconscious and intense desire for attention and approval from others. This can manifest as flamboyant behavior, a need to be the center of attention, and a tendency to seek reassurance and validation in social interactions.

Coping Mechanisms for Insecurity:

The attention-seeking behaviors associated with HPD can serve as a coping mechanism for underlying feelings of insecurity and inadequacy. By garnering attention, individuals with HPD may temporarily alleviate their internal doubts and anxieties.

Emotional Instability and Shifting Identity

Rapidly shifting and shallow expression of emotions in HPD may be linked to difficulties in maintaining a stable sense of self. Individuals with HPD may rely on external validation to define their identity, leading to emotional volatility based on the reactions and responses of others.

Interpersonal Sensitivity and Suggestibility:

Individuals with HPD often display a high level of interpersonal sensitivity and suggestibility. They might be susceptible to the feelings and opinions of others, which would further influence their own actions and expressions.

Fear of Abandonment:

The fear of being ignored or abandoned is a common theme in HPD. This fear can drive individuals to engage in attention-seeking behaviors as a means of securing connections and avoiding perceived rejection.

Fantasy and Escapism:

The use of theatrical and dramatic elements in communication and behavior may serve as a form of escapism. Creating a fantastical or exaggerated self-presentation allows individuals with HPD to temporarily distance themselves from underlying emotional challenges.

Early life influences and developmental factors

Early life influences and developmental factors play a significant role in shaping the emergence of histrionic personality disorder

(HPD). Several key elements contribute to the development of this personality disorder:

Parental Relationships:

The quality of early attachments and relationships with caregivers can influence the development of HPD. Inconsistent or overly demanding caregiving, as well as a lack of emotional attunement, may contribute to the individual's later need for external validation and attention.

Modeling Behavior:

Children often model their behavior based on the significant figures in their lives. If they observe attention-seeking or dramatic behaviors in their caregivers or other influential individuals, they may adopt similar strategies to fulfill their emotional needs.

Reinforcement of Attention-Seeking Behaviors:

Early experiences that reinforce attention-seeking behaviors, such as receiving praise or positive attention for dramatic actions, can contribute to the development of HPD. The individual learns that such behaviors are effective in gaining the desired response from others.

Invalidation and rejection:

Experiences of invalidation, rejection, or perceived neglect during early development may lead individuals to develop maladaptive coping mechanisms. Seeking attention becomes a way to counteract feelings of rejection and fill emotional voids.

Identity Formation Challenges:

Difficulties in forming a stable sense of self during childhood may contribute to the need for external validation. If an individual's identity is not adequately supported or encouraged, they may rely on attention and approval from others to define themselves.

Family Dynamics:

Dysfunctional family dynamics, such as overprotectiveness or inconsistent discipline, can contribute to the development of HPD. A family environment that prioritizes appearances and places a high value on external validation may contribute to the formation of histrionic traits.

Cultural and social influences:

Societal and cultural factors can also play a role in shaping early development. Cultural expectations regarding gender roles, expressions of emotion, and interpersonal interactions may influence the emergence of histrionic traits.

Temperamental Factors:

Certain temperamental traits, such as high sensitivity to social cues or a natural inclination toward extraversion, may interact with early experiences to contribute to the development of HPD. Individuals with a predisposition to seek social approval may be more susceptible to developing histrionic traits.

Parental Expectations and Pressure:

Unrealistic expectations or intense pressure from parents to achieve certain standards may lead to a heightened need for external validation. Children who grow up in an environment where their worth is closely tied to achievements or appearances may develop histrionic traits as a way to meet these expectations.

Sibling Dynamics:

Interactions with siblings can also influence the development of HPD. Sibling rivalry or a dynamic where attention is unevenly distributed may contribute to a heightened desire for attention and approval in an individual with histrionic traits.

Social learning and peer relationships:

Peer relationships and social interactions during childhood and adolescence are crucial in shaping personality development. If an individual experiences difficulties forming peer connections or perceives a lack of popularity, they may turn to attention-seeking behaviors as a way to gain social acceptance.

Traumatic Experiences:

Early traumatic experiences, such as abuse or neglect, can contribute to the development of HPD as a coping mechanism. Seeking attention and approval may serve as a way to navigate feelings of vulnerability and powerlessness associated with past traumas.

Parental Modeling of Emotional Expression:

The way parents express and manage their own emotions can impact how a child learns to regulate and express emotions. If a parent demonstrates dramatic or attention-seeking behaviors, a child may internalize similar ways of relating to others.

Recognizing the complex interplay of these early life influences and developmental factors is essential for mental health professionals to tailor interventions that address the unique circumstances of individuals with histrionic personality disorder. By addressing these underlying dynamics, therapeutic approaches can work towards fostering healthier patterns of self-expression, interpersonal relationships, and emotional regulation.

Neurobiological Considerations

Neurobiological considerations in histrionic personality disorder (HPD) involve exploring how brain structure, function, and neurotransmitter systems may contribute to the manifestation of this personality disorder. While research in this area is ongoing and not yet fully elucidated, several aspects are worth considering:

Brain Structure and Function:

Neuroimaging studies suggest that alterations in brain structure and function may be associated with personality disorders. In the case of HPD, regions involved in emotional processing, such as the amygdala and prefrontal cortex, could play a role in the intense emotional expressions and impulsivity seen in individuals with this disorder.

Neurotransmitter Systems:

Imbalances in neurotransmitter systems, including serotonin, dopamine, and norepinephrine, have been implicated in various personality disorders. These neurotransmitters play a crucial role in regulating mood, impulsivity, and attention, and their dysregulation may contribute to the emotional volatility and attention-seeking behaviors observed in HPD.

Genetic Factors:

There is evidence to suggest a genetic component in the development of personality disorders, including HPD. Genetic factors may influence the temperament and emotional reactivity of individuals, contributing to the predisposition for attention-seeking behaviors and the need for external validation.

Environmental Influences on Brain Development:

Early environmental factors, such as childhood adversity and trauma, can impact brain development. Stressful experiences during critical periods of brain development may shape neural circuits involved in emotional regulation and social behavior, potentially contributing to the features observed in HPD.

Reward Processing:

The neurobiological basis of reward processing may be relevant to understanding attention-seeking behaviors. Dysregulation in the brain's reward system could contribute to the persistent need for external reinforcement and approval seen in individuals with HPD.

Neuroplasticity:

The brain's ability to adapt and change, known as neuroplasticity, could be relevant to the development and maintenance of personality disorders. Interventions targeting maladaptive patterns of thinking and behavior may influence neuroplasticity, promoting more adaptive neural pathways.

It's important to note that the field of neurobiology and personality disorders is complex, and research is ongoing to unravel the specific neurobiological underpinnings of HPD. The interplay between genetic predisposition, early life experiences, and neurobiological factors likely contributes to the heterogeneity of presentations observed in individuals with histrionic personality disorder. Advances in neuroscience may provide further insights into potential targets for therapeutic interventions in the future.

Co-occurring conditions and comorbidities

Histrionic Personality Disorder (HPD) often coexists with other mental health conditions, known as comorbidities. The presence of these comorbidities can complicate the clinical picture and influence the course and treatment of HPD. Some common co-occurring conditions include:

Mood Disorders:

Individuals with HPD may experience comorbid mood disorders such as depression or bipolar disorder. The intense emotional expression and rapid mood shifts characteristic of HPD can overlap with symptoms of mood disorders.

Anxiety Disorders:

Anxiety disorders, including generalized anxiety disorder or social anxiety disorder, may co-occur with HPD. The need for approval and fear of rejection seen in HPD can contribute to heightened levels of anxiety in social situations.

Somatization Disorders:

People with HPD may experience somatic symptoms and physical health worries that are difficult to explain by a medical condition. This overlap may lead to comorbid somatic symptom disorders.

Eating Disorders:

There is an increased risk of co-occurring eating disorders, such as bulimia nervosa or binge eating disorder, in individuals with HPD. The emphasis on physical appearance and the desire for attention can contribute to disordered eating behaviors.

Substance Use Disorders:

Substance use disorders may coexist with HPD, especially in individuals using substances as a way to cope with emotional dysregulation or to enhance social experiences. The impulsive and sensation-seeking nature of HPD may contribute to substance misuse.

Other personality disorders:

HPD can overlap with other personality disorders, creating a complex clinical presentation. For example, features of narcissistic personality disorder or borderline personality disorder may be observed alongside HPD.

Attention-Deficit/Hyperactivity Disorder (ADHD):

ADHD symptoms, such as impulsivity and difficulty sustaining attention, may co-occur with HPD. These overlapping features can impact an individual's ability to regulate behavior and engage in goal-directed activities.

Relationship Issues:

Difficulties in forming and maintaining stable relationships are inherent in HPD. Relationship issues may contribute to comorbid conditions such as marital distress or family conflicts.

Chapter Three

Case Study 1: Overcoming Social Challenges

Case Study: Overcoming Social Challenges in Histrionic Personality Disorder (HPD)

Background:

Alice, a 30-year-old woman, presented with symptoms indicative of histrionic personality disorder (HPD). She struggled with an intense fear of social rejection and had a persistent need for attention. These traits affected her ability to form and maintain meaningful relationships and created challenges in both her personal and professional lives.

Intervention:

A multidimensional approach was implemented to address Alice's social challenges:

Psychoeducation:

Alice received psychoeducation on histrionic personality disorder, helping her understand the underlying factors contributing to her social challenges. This increased her self-awareness and facilitated a foundation for change.

Cognitive-Behavioral Therapy (CBT):

CBT was employed to target maladaptive thought patterns and behaviors. Alice learned to identify and challenge negative beliefs about herself and others. Strategies were developed to shift her focus from seeking constant approval to developing a more realistic and balanced self-perception.

Social skills training:

To enhance her interpersonal skills, Alice participated in social skills training. This involved practicing effective communication, active listening, and understanding social cues. Role-playing exercises helped her navigate various social scenarios with increased confidence.

Gradual Exposure:

Alice engaged in gradual exposure exercises to confront her fear of social situations. Starting with less anxiety-provoking scenarios, she systematically faced and navigated progressively challenging social interactions. This desensitization process helped reduce her social anxiety.

Mindfulness and Emotional Regulation:

Mindfulness techniques were incorporated to help Alice regulate her intense emotions. Mindfulness practices allowed her to become more aware of her emotional responses and implement healthier coping mechanisms, reducing impulsive reactions in social settings.

Progress:

Over the course of therapy, Alice showed significant progress. She reported increased comfort in social situations, improved communication with peers, and a notable reduction in attention-seeking behaviors. The development of a supportive social network contributed to her enhanced sense of self-worth and reduced reliance on external validation.

Follow-up:

Regular follow-up sessions focused on maintaining progress, reinforcing newly acquired skills, and addressing any residual challenges. Alice's continued commitment to self-improvement and the therapeutic process contributed to sustained positive outcomes.

This case study highlights the effectiveness of a comprehensive therapeutic approach in addressing the social challenges associated with histrionic personality disorder, emphasizing psychoeducation, cognitive-behavioral strategies, and skill-building exercises.

Challenges and Breakthroughs:

Despite progress, challenges emerged during therapy, particularly during moments of stress or perceived social threat. Alice faced setbacks when encountering situations that triggered her fear of rejection. These instances became opportunities for deeper exploration and refinement of coping strategies. The therapeutic process involved helping Alice recognize these challenges as part of her ongoing journey rather than as failures.

Integration of Support Systems:

A crucial aspect of Alice's progress involved integrating support systems. Involving close friends or family members in certain therapy sessions helped bridge the gap between therapeutic insights and real-world application. This collaborative approach facilitated a more comprehensive understanding of Alice's interpersonal dynamics and contributed to a more supportive social environment.

Career and Professional Growth:

Addressing the impact of HPD on Alice's professional life was another pivotal aspect of her treatment. Through targeted interventions, including workplace communication strategies and stress management techniques, Alice navigated challenges in her career more effectively. This not only improved her job satisfaction but also provided additional opportunities for positive social interactions.

Maintaining Gains and Future Outlook:

As therapy progressed, the focus shifted towards maintaining gains and preparing Alice for the future. Building resilience against potential setbacks, identifying early warning signs of maladaptive behaviors, and reinforcing a positive self-image became integral to sustaining the progress achieved.

Holistic Well-being:

The holistic approach to Alice's treatment extended beyond symptom reduction. The emphasis was placed on fostering a sense of holistic well-being, including physical health, self-care practices, and the pursuit of personal interests. These aspects contributed to a more balanced and fulfilling life, reducing the reliance on external validation as the primary source of satisfaction.

Conclusion:

Alice's journey exemplifies the transformative potential of a comprehensive therapeutic approach to addressing the social challenges associated with histrionic personality disorder. Through psychoeducation, skill-building, and ongoing support, she not only overcame social obstacles but also experienced significant personal growth. This case underscores the importance of tailored interventions that consider the unique needs and strengths of individuals with HPD, offering a roadmap for navigating the complexities of social interactions and achieving meaningful change.

Case Study 2: Transformative Therapeutic Journeys

Case Study 2: Transformative Therapeutic Journeys in Histrionic Personality Disorder (HPD)

Background:

John, a 28-year-old man, sought therapy for difficulties in forming and maintaining relationships. He exhibited characteristics consistent with histrionic personality disorder (HPD), including a pervasive need for attention, emotional expressiveness, and challenges in establishing deep connections.

Intervention:

John's therapeutic journey involved a multifaceted approach to address the core aspects of HPD:

Exploration of Early Experiences:

The therapeutic process began with an exploration of John's early experiences and attachment patterns. Insights into childhood dynamics and the influence of parental relationships helped illuminate the roots of his attention-seeking behaviors.

Mindfulness-Based Techniques:

Mindfulness practices were introduced to enhance John's emotional regulation and self-awareness. Mindfulness exercises allowed him to observe and understand his emotional responses without being overwhelmed, fostering a greater sense of control.

Interpersonal Effectiveness Training:

John participated in interpersonal effectiveness training to refine his communication skills and navigate social interactions more effectively. This involved assertiveness training, active listening exercises, and strategies to express emotions in a balanced manner.

Exploration of Core Beliefs:

Cognitive-behavioral interventions focused on identifying and challenging John's core beliefs about himself and relationships. Addressing cognitive distortions helped him develop more realistic and adaptive thought patterns, reducing the need for constant validation.

Individual and group therapy:

John engaged in both individual and group therapy sessions. Individual therapy provided a space for personal exploration and tailored interventions, while group therapy allowed him to practice interpersonal skills in a supportive environment, gaining feedback from peers.

Progress:

Over the course of therapy, John demonstrated significant progress in various domains. He reported a decrease in attention-seeking behaviors, improved emotional regulation, and enhanced interpersonal connections. The combination of insight-oriented approaches and skill-building interventions contributed to John's transformative journey.

Creative Expression as a Therapeutic Tool:

Recognizing John's inclination towards creative expression, therapy incorporated art and narrative techniques. This allowed him to express emotions, fears, and aspirations in a non-verbal and symbolic manner, providing additional avenues for self-discovery and reflection.

Integration of Relational Patterns:

Therapy delved into John's relational patterns, emphasizing the importance of forming authentic connections. By exploring the quality of his relationships and addressing patterns of idealization or devaluation, John gained a deeper understanding of how he related to others.

Post-Therapy Maintenance:

As therapy approached its conclusion, a maintenance plan was developed to support John's continued growth. This included strategies for self-monitoring, coping with potential setbacks, and integrating the skills acquired in therapy into daily life.

Conclusion:

John's transformative therapeutic journey illustrates the efficacy of a tailored, integrative approach to addressing the complexities of histrionic personality disorder. By combining insight-oriented exploration with skill-building interventions and creative expression, therapy not only targeted symptom reduction but also fostered lasting personal growth and improved relational dynamics. This case underscores the importance of adapting therapeutic strategies to individual strengths and preferences, providing a template for navigating the intricate terrain of HPD.

John's journey further involved exploring his intimate relationships. Collaborative interventions included couples counseling, where both partners participated in sessions to enhance communication and understanding. This provided a platform to address relational challenges and strengthen the foundation of meaningful connections.

Workplace Integration:

Recognizing the impact of HPD on John's professional life, therapy was extended to the workplace. Interventions focused on effective communication in a professional setting, stress management strategies, and establishing healthy boundaries. John's newfound skills contributed to improved workplace dynamics and job satisfaction.

Social Integration and Community Engagement:

A crucial aspect of John's therapeutic journey was extending beyond the individual and interpersonal realms to address social integration. Encouraging participation in community activities, clubs, or volunteer work provided opportunities for John to practice social skills in diverse settings, fostering a sense of belonging beyond personal relationships.

Long-Term Planning and Relapse Prevention:

The concluding phase of therapy involved developing a long-term plan and relapse prevention strategies. John actively participated in creating a roadmap for sustaining progress independently, including ongoing self-reflection, continued skill reinforcement, and utilizing support systems.

Peer Support and Networking:

Recognizing the importance of social support, John was encouraged to build a network of peers who understood and supported his journey. Peer support groups offered a platform for sharing experiences, coping strategies, and mutual encouragement.

Post-Therapy Reflection:

As John reflected on his therapeutic journey, he acknowledged the profound changes in his self-perception and relationships. The therapeutic process not only addressed the symptomatic aspects of HPD but also empowered him to navigate life with increased self-awareness and adaptive coping mechanisms.

Integration of Positive Reinforcement:

Positive reinforcement played a pivotal role in sustaining progress. Celebrating milestones, both big and small, reinforced John's commitment to growth and provided a foundation for continued resilience in the face of future challenges.

Conclusion:

John's transformative therapeutic journey exemplifies the holistic and collaborative nature of addressing histrionic personality disorder. By integrating individual exploration, interpersonal interventions, workplace strategies, and community engagement, therapy extends beyond symptom reduction to facilitate enduring personal growth. This case underscores the dynamic and evolving nature of therapeutic journeys, offering valuable insights into the multifaceted approach needed to navigate the complexities of HPD and foster meaningful change.

Case Study 3: Building Resilience in Everyday Life

Case Study 3: Building Resilience in Everyday Life with Histrionic Personality Disorder (HPD)

Background:

Sarah, a 32-year-old woman, sought therapy for challenges associated with histrionic personality disorder (HPD). She grappled with a persistent need for attention, intense emotional expression, and difficulties in forming lasting relationships.

Intervention:

Sarah's therapeutic journey focused on building resilience in everyday life, incorporating the following elements:

Strengths-Based Approach:

Therapy began with a strengths-based assessment, identifying Sarah's unique qualities and positive attributes. Emphasizing these strengths provided a foundation for cultivating resilience and self-esteem.

Narrative Therapy Techniques:

Narrative therapy techniques were employed to explore and reconstruct Sarah's self-narrative. By reframing her life story in a more empowering light, she gained a sense of agency and control over her experiences, contributing to increased resilience.

Mindfulness and Emotional Regulation:

Mindfulness practices were integrated to enhance Sarah's emotional regulation. Mindful awareness of her thoughts and feelings allowed her to respond to situations with greater calmness and clarity, reducing the impulsive reactions associated with HPD.

Graded Exposure and Social Skills Building:

Graded exposure exercises were introduced to help Sarah gradually confront social situations that triggered anxiety. Simultaneously, social skills building focused on effective communication, active listening, and interpreting social cues to enhance her capacity to navigate relationships.

Progress:

Through consistent effort and the integration of resilience-building strategies, Sarah demonstrated notable progress:

Increased emotional resilience:

Sarah developed increased emotional resilience, responding to setbacks with greater adaptability and maintaining a more stable emotional state.

Improved social functioning:

Social skills training contributed to improved social functioning. Sarah reported feeling more at ease in social interactions, forming connections based on genuine communication rather than relying solely on attention-seeking behaviors.

Reduced Impulsivity:

Mindfulness practices played a pivotal role in reducing impulsive behaviors. Sarah learned to pause and reflect before reacting, contributing to healthier interpersonal dynamics.

Integration into Daily Life:

As therapy progressed, the focus shifted towards integrating resilience-building strategies into Sarah's daily life.

Self-Care Practices:

Sarah established self-care practices that aligned with her interests and preferences, promoting overall well-being and providing a buffer against stressors.

Journaling and Reflection:

Journaling became a tool for self-reflection. Sarah documented her emotional experiences, challenges, and triumphs, fostering a deeper understanding of herself and her journey.

Community Engagement:

Encouraging Sarah to engage with community activities and support networks further bolstered her resilience. Participation in group activities provided opportunities for social connection and a sense of belonging.

Exploring Personal Goals:

The therapeutic process with Sarah delved into the exploration of personal goals and aspirations. Collaboratively setting realistic and meaningful goals provided Sarah with a sense of purpose and direction. This goal-oriented approach allowed her to channel her energy and attention toward constructive endeavors, contributing to a more fulfilling life.

Building a Supportive Social Network:

Recognizing the significance of social support, Sarah actively worked on building a supportive social network. The therapeutic journey involved identifying individuals who valued her for more than attention-seeking behaviors. Strengthening connections with friends who appreciated her authentic self provided a vital source of encouragement and understanding.

Navigating Romantic Relationships:

A particular focus of therapy was navigating romantic relationships. Sarah's desire for intense connections sometimes led to challenges in forming and maintaining stable partnerships. Through relationship-focused interventions, she gained insights into healthy relationship dynamics, fostering a more balanced and sustainable approach to romantic involvement.

Creative Expression as an Outlet:

Given Sarah's affinity for creative expression, therapy incorporated avenues for artistic outlets. Engaging in activities such as art, writing, or music provided Sarah with a constructive channel for emotional expression, enabling her to channel intense emotions into creative endeavors.

Post-Therapy Transition:

As therapy neared its conclusion, a transitional phase was implemented. This involved gradually reducing the frequency of sessions while maintaining ongoing support mechanisms. Sarah's newfound resilience and coping skills were reinforced, empowering her to apply these strategies independently.

Integration of Resilience into Identity:

A crucial aspect of the post-therapy phase was the integration of resilience into Sarah's identity. Resilience-building became an intrinsic part of how she approached challenges, fostering a mindset that embraced growth, adaptability, and self-compassion.

Community Involvement and Advocacy:

Sarah's journey extended beyond personal growth to community involvement and advocacy. Drawing from her experiences, she expressed a desire to contribute to mental health awareness. This newfound sense of purpose led to her involvement in local community initiatives, where she shared her journey to inspire others facing similar challenges.

Long-Term Outlook:

Sarah's case illustrates the enduring impact of a resilience-focused therapeutic approach on individuals with histrionic personality disorder. The emphasis on strengths, goal-setting, and community engagement provided a roadmap for sustained personal growth. Sarah had a proactive outlook on life, one that was characterized by resiliency, meaningful connections, and a dedication to ongoing self-discovery.

Strengths-Based Approaches:

A strengths-based approach proved instrumental in fostering resilience. Recognizing and building upon an individual's strengths provides a solid foundation for personal growth, empowering them to overcome challenges associated with HPD.

Mindfulness and Emotional Regulation:

The integration of mindfulness practices offers valuable tools for emotional regulation. Mindfulness not only reduces impulsivity but also enhances self-awareness, enabling individuals to navigate social situations with greater composure and thoughtfulness.

Goal-Setting and Purpose:

Setting realistic and meaningful goals plays a pivotal role in the therapeutic journey. Personal aspirations provide direction and purpose, motivating individuals to actively engage in their own growth and pursue a fulfilling life.

Creative Expression as a Therapeutic Outlet:

Incorporating creative expression as a therapeutic outlet taps into the unique strengths and preferences of individuals. Artistic endeavors offer a constructive channel for emotional expression and self-discovery, contributing to the overall well-being of individuals with HPD.

Community Connection and Advocacy:

Community involvement and advocacy create a sense of belonging and purpose. Sharing one's journey can inspire others, reduce stigma, and contribute to a supportive community where individuals with HPD feel understood and accepted.

Resilience as a Core Identity Trait:

Resilience-building is not just a set of skills but a core identity trait. Integrating resilience into one's self-concept empowers individuals to face life's challenges with adaptability, bounce back from setbacks, and maintain a positive outlook.

Ongoing Self-Reflection and Growth:

The journey with histrionic personality disorder is ongoing and requires a commitment to self-reflection and growth. Regular self-check-ins, continued therapy or support, and a willingness to adapt strategies contribute to sustained well-being.

Chapter Four

Understanding Relationship Dynamics with HPD

Understanding relationship dynamics with Histrionic Personality Disorder (HPD) involves recognizing the unique challenges and characteristics that individuals with HPD may bring to interpersonal connections. Here are key insights into relationship dynamics with HPD:

Intense Desire for Attention:

Individuals with HPD often have a pervasive and intense desire for attention. This may manifest in seeking constant reassurance, becoming the center of social interactions, and displaying dramatic or flamboyant behaviors to capture attention.

Rapidly Shifting Emotions:

Emotional expression in individuals with HPD can be rapid and intense. This emotional volatility may lead to frequent mood swings and difficulties in maintaining emotional stability, impacting the overall dynamics of relationships.

Dependence on External Validation:

A core feature of HPD is the reliance on external validation for self-worth. This dependence on others for approval can create challenges in forming authentic connections, as the individual may prioritize pleasing others over expressing their true selves.

Difficulty Maintaining Boundaries:

Individuals with HPD may struggle with maintaining appropriate emotional and physical boundaries in relationships. This can lead to a blurring of lines between personal and interpersonal space, impacting the comfort level of those involved.

Idealization and Devaluation:

Relationship dynamics with HPD may follow a pattern of idealization and devaluation. Individuals with HPD may initially idealize others, viewing them as perfect, but may later become disappointed or disillusioned, leading to abrupt changes in their perception of the relationship.

Challenges in Forming Long-Term Relationships:

Establishing and maintaining long-term relationships can be challenging for individuals with HPD. The intense need for novelty and excitement may lead to a pattern of short-lived relationships as sustained attention and interest become difficult to maintain.

Impulsivity in Decision-Making:

Impulsivity is a common trait in HPD, and this can extend to decision-making within relationships. Individuals with HPD may make impulsive choices that impact the relationship, leading to unpredictability and potential instability.

Conflict Avoidance or Escalation:

Relationship conflicts with individuals with HPD may be approached in two ways: either through extreme efforts to avoid conflict to maintain harmony or through intense emotional reactions and escalation. This dichotomy can contribute to difficulties in resolving issues effectively.

Interpersonal Sensitivity:

Despite the challenges, individuals with HPD often possess heightened interpersonal sensitivity. They may be adept at picking up on social cues and adjusting their behavior to gain attention or approval, making them socially intuitive.

Communication Challenges:

The individual's need for constant attention and validation may have an impact on communication dynamics in relationships with HPD. They may prioritize expressing themselves dramatically, potentially overshadowing the perspectives and needs of others. Effective communication strategies that promote active listening and mutual understanding are essential in navigating these challenges.

Addressing Fear of Abandonment:

The fear of abandonment is a common underlying theme in HPD. Individuals with HPD may engage in behaviors to prevent perceived abandonment, such as clinging excessively to partners or becoming excessively reactive to signs of potential rejection. This fear can impact stability and trust within relationships.

Navigating Jealousy and Competition:

Jealousy and competition for attention may arise in relationships involving HPD. Individuals may perceive others as rivals for attention, leading to interpersonal conflicts. Strategies for addressing and managing jealousy, fostering open communication, and building trust are crucial components of relationship dynamics with HPD.

Encouraging Individual Identity:

Relationships with HPD can benefit from encouraging and maintaining individual identities. Balancing the need for attention and validation with the importance of personal autonomy allows for healthier and more sustainable connections. Partnerships that celebrate each person's uniqueness contribute to a more robust relationship foundation.

Setting Clear Expectations:

Establishing clear expectations within the relationship is vital. Both partners benefit from open communication about needs, boundaries, and the level of attention each is comfortable providing. Setting realistic expectations helps manage potential conflicts and fosters a more secure relationship environment.

Role of Empathy and Understanding:

Developing empathy and understanding is crucial for both individuals with HPD and their partners. Recognizing and validating each other's emotions and needs fosters a sense of connection and helps navigate the challenges that may arise in the relationship.

Therapeutic Support:

Couples therapy or relationship counseling can be valuable resources for individuals with HPD and their partners. A skilled therapist can facilitate open communication, provide tools for conflict resolution, and offer guidance in navigating the unique dynamics associated with Histrionic Personality Disorder.

Personal and Relationship Growth:

Relationships involving HPD provide opportunities for personal and relational growth. Partners can learn to navigate challenges collaboratively, fostering resilience and adaptability. The journey towards growth involves a shared commitment to understanding, supporting, and adapting to the evolving dynamics of the relationship.

Cultivating Emotional Resilience:

Emotional resilience is a key component in navigating relationships with HPD. Both individuals can benefit from cultivating resilience to manage the ups and downs of emotional intensity, fostering a more stable and supportive partnership.

Communication Strategies for Partners and Loved Ones

Effective communication is crucial when navigating relationships with individuals who have Histrionic Personality Disorder (HPD). Here are communication strategies for partners and loved ones:

Active Listening:

Practice active listening to fully understand the individual's thoughts and feelings. Give them your full attention, maintain eye contact, and provide verbal and non-verbal cues to show that you are engaged in the conversation.

Validate Emotions:

Acknowledge and validate the emotions expressed by the individual. Recognize their feelings without judgment, even if you may not fully understand or agree with them. Validation fosters a sense of being heard and understood.

Express Boundaries Clearly:

Clearly communicate your own boundaries within the relationship. Be assertive about what you are comfortable with and what behaviors may be challenging for you. Establishing clear boundaries helps create a more stable and respectful dynamic.

Use "I" Statements:

Frame your concerns or needs using "I" statements to avoid sounding accusatory. For example, say, "I feel overwhelmed when there is a lot of drama," rather than, "You always create drama." This helps you express your perspective without triggering defensiveness.

Set Realistic Expectations:

Communicate and set realistic expectations for the relationship. Clearly define roles, responsibilities, and expectations to avoid misunderstandings. Having a shared understanding of what each person brings to the relationship can help manage potential conflicts.

Provide Positive Reinforcement:

Offer positive reinforcement when the individual displays behaviors that align with healthy communication and interpersonal skills. Reinforce positive aspects of the relationship to encourage continued growth and positive interactions.

Encourage Open Dialogue:

Create an environment that encourages open dialogue. Let the individual know that their thoughts and feelings are valued and that you are open to discussing concerns or challenges as they arise. This promotes transparency and trust.

Avoid Power Struggles:

Refrain from engaging in power struggles or attempts to control the individual. Instead, focus on collaborative problem-solving and finding common ground. Mutual understanding and compromise contribute to a more harmonious relationship.

Address Concerns Calmly:

If concerns or conflicts arise, address them calmly and constructively. Avoid responding impulsively to emotional intensity. Take time to process your own emotions before engaging in discussions about sensitive topics.

Be Patient and Understanding:

Encourage Professional Support:

Suggest and support the idea of seeking professional help, such as therapy or counseling. A mental health professional can provide additional tools and strategies to navigate the challenges associated with Histrionic Personality Disorder.

Celebrate Achievements:

Celebrate achievements and positive changes in the individual's behavior. Reinforce the progress made in developing healthier communication patterns and building a more stable relationship.

Effective communication requires ongoing effort and a commitment to understanding each other's perspectives. By incorporating these strategies, partners and loved ones can foster a more supportive and resilient connection with individuals with Histrionic Personality Disorder.

Encourage Emotional Expression:

Create a safe space for the individual to express their emotions. Encourage them to share their feelings openly and without fear of judgment. This can promote a deeper emotional connection and help them feel understood.

Discuss Communication Preferences:

Have an open conversation about communication preferences. Understand how the individual prefers to receive feedback and discuss concerns. Clarifying communication styles can prevent misunderstandings and enhance the overall quality of interactions.

Seek Mutual Solutions:

Approach challenges as a team and seek mutual solutions. Collaborative problem-solving encourages a sense of partnership and reinforces the idea that both individuals are actively working towards a healthier relationship.

Educate Yourself About HPD:

Take the initiative to educate yourself about Histrionic Personality Disorder. Understanding the specific traits, triggers, and challenges associated with HPD can provide valuable insights into the individual's behavior, fostering empathy and informed communication.

Foster Independence:

Encourage the development of independence and self-confidence. Acknowledge and celebrate the individual's achievements and strengths. Fostering a sense of self-worth independent of external validation can contribute to a more balanced dynamic.

Create Rituals of Connection:

Establish rituals of connection that promote positive interactions. Whether it's a regular check-in, shared activities, or moments of celebration, creating consistent and positive rituals strengthens the emotional bond in the relationship.

Navigate Attention-Seeking Behaviors:

Approach attention-seeking behaviors with understanding and compassion. Instead of responding with frustration, explore the underlying needs that drive these behaviors. Discuss healthier ways to fulfill those needs within the context of the relationship.

Clarify Intentions and Feelings:

Clarify intentions and feelings to avoid misunderstandings. Clearly communicate your own intentions and ask for clarification when needed. Misinterpretations can lead to unnecessary conflicts, so fostering clarity is essential.

Celebrate Individual Identities:

Acknowledge and celebrate each other's individual identities within the relationship. Emphasize the importance of maintaining personal interests, friendships, and goals. This contributes to a more dynamic and fulfilling connection.

Create a Supportive Network:

Establish a supportive network for both partners. Engage with friends, family, or support groups who understand the unique dynamics of the relationship. Having a supportive community provides additional resources for navigating challenges.

Reflect on Progress Regularly:

Set aside time to reflect on the progress made in the relationship. Celebrate positive changes and discuss ongoing goals. Regular reflection reinforces the commitment to growth and encourages a forward-focused mindset.

Practice Self-Care:

Prioritize self-care for both partners. Taking care of individual well-being contributes to a healthier relationship dynamic. Encourage activities that promote relaxation, stress reduction, and overall emotional well-being.

Maintain Flexibility:

Recognize that flexibility is key to navigating the complexities of HPD. Be open to adapting communication strategies and relationship dynamics as needed. Flexibility fosters resilience and allows for ongoing growth and connection.

Building effective communication in relationships involving Histrionic Personality Disorder requires patience, understanding, and a commitment to mutual growth. By incorporating these strategies, partners and loved ones can contribute to a more positive and fulfilling relationship dynamic.

Supporting Friends and Family: A Guide

Supporting Friends and Family: A Guide to Navigating Histrionic Personality Disorder (HPD)

Supporting someone with Histrionic Personality Disorder (HPD) requires compassion, understanding, and effective communication. Here's a guide to help friends and family navigate the complexities of HPD:

Educate Yourself:

Take the time to educate yourself about Histrionic Personality Disorder. Understanding the traits, challenges, and triggers associated with HPD can provide valuable insights into your loved one's behavior.

Practice Empathy:

Approach your loved one with empathy. Recognize that their emotions may be intense and that they may struggle with seeking validation. Empathy creates a foundation for understanding and fosters a supportive environment.

Active Listening:

Practice active listening when your loved one wants to share their thoughts and feelings. Offer your full attention, refrain from judgment, and validate their emotions. Active listening reinforces the idea that their experiences are valued.

Establish Clear Communication:

Establish clear communication about your own boundaries and needs. Openly discuss what you are comfortable with and work together to find common ground. Clear communication helps create a more stable and respectful dynamic.

Encourage Professional Help:

Encourage your loved one to seek professional help, such as therapy or counseling. A mental health professional can provide additional tools and strategies to manage HPD, fostering personal growth and improved relationships.

Provide Positive Reinforcement:

Offer positive reinforcement when you observe healthy behaviors. Reinforce positive aspects of their personality and actions, promoting a sense of accomplishment and encouraging continued growth.

Support Individual Interests:

Encourage the pursuit of individual interests and activities. Supporting your loved one's passions and hobbies contributes to a sense of fulfillment and helps them maintain a sense of identity outside of the disorder.

Set Realistic Expectations:

Set realistic expectations for the relationship. Clearly communicate your expectations and be open to finding compromises. Realistic expectations contribute to a more harmonious and understanding connection.

Respond with Calmness:

Respond to intense emotions with calmness and understanding. Avoid reacting impulsively to emotional intensity, and instead, offer support and reassurance. Responding with calmness helps de-escalate potentially challenging situations.

Be Patient and Flexible:

Patience is key when supporting someone with HPD. Recognize that personal growth is a gradual process, and setbacks may occur.

Stay flexible and adapt your approach based on your loved one's changing needs.

Celebrate Achievements:

Celebrate achievements and positive changes. Acknowledge and celebrate the progress made in managing HPD symptoms and building healthier communication patterns.

Join Supportive Communities:

Seek support for yourself by joining communities or support groups for friends and family of individuals with HPD. Sharing experiences and strategies with others in similar situations can provide valuable insights and encouragement.

Encourage Self-Care:

Promote self-care for both you and your loved one. Encourage activities that foster relaxation, stress reduction, and overall well-being. Taking care of individual well-being contributes to a healthier relationship dynamic.

Address Misunderstandings Tactfully:

Address misunderstandings tactfully and openly. If conflicts arise, approach them with understanding and a desire to find resolutions.

Tactful communication helps prevent unnecessary tension in the relationship.

Professional Perspectives on Relationship Building

Express Unconditional Love:

Express unconditional love and acceptance. Communicate that your support is not contingent on specific behaviors but is rooted in your love for the person. Unconditional love fosters a sense of security and trust.

Supporting a loved one with Histrionic Personality Disorder is a journey that requires ongoing commitment and understanding. By incorporating these strategies, you contribute to creating a supportive environment that fosters personal growth and positive relationships.

Encourage Healthy Relationships:

Offer guidance on cultivating healthy relationships. Help your loved one understand the importance of balanced connections built on mutual respect and understanding. Encouraging healthier relationship dynamics supports their overall well-being.

Model Effective Communication:

Model effective communication in your interactions. Demonstrate active listening, assertiveness, and empathy. By embodying healthy communication, you provide a positive example for your loved one to learn from and emulate.

Involve Them in Decision-Making:

Involve your loved one in decision-making processes when appropriate. Providing them with a sense of agency and input fosters a feeling of being valued and included in important aspects of life.

Collaborate on Coping Strategies:

Collaborate on coping strategies for managing intense emotions. Work together to identify healthy coping mechanisms that can be implemented during challenging moments. This collaborative approach empowers your loved one to take an active role in their emotional well-being.

Celebrate Individual Growth:

Celebrate moments of individual growth and self-discovery. Acknowledge and appreciate the efforts your loved one is making to understand themselves better and develop healthier patterns of behavior.

Engage in Shared Activities:

Engage in shared activities that bring joy and build positive memories. Participating in activities together fosters a sense of connection and provides opportunities for shared experiences that go beyond the challenges associated with HPD.

Encourage Routine and Stability:

Advocate for routine and stability in daily life. Establishing a sense of predictability can be comforting for individuals with HPD and can contribute to emotional regulation. Encourage the development of a routine that includes self-care practices.

Promote Emotional Intelligence:

Promote the development of emotional intelligence. Encourage your loved one to explore and understand their emotions, fostering a greater awareness of their emotional landscape. Emotional intelligence contributes to improved self-regulation and interpersonal skills

Provide Resources for Self-Help:

Offer resources for self-help and personal development. Recommend books, articles, or online resources that focus on building emotional resilience, healthy relationships, and self-improvement. Empowering your loved one with knowledge enhances their capacity for growth.

Discuss Future Planning:

Engage in discussions about future planning collaboratively. Address aspirations, goals, and plans for personal and relational growth. Planning for the future can instill a sense of purpose and direction, motivating positive changes.

Maintain Open Lines of Communication:

Keep communication channels open and encourage ongoing dialogue. Create an atmosphere where your loved one feels comfortable sharing their thoughts and concerns. Regular communication facilitates understanding and strengthens your connection.

Acknowledge Efforts Towards Change:

Acknowledge and appreciate any efforts your loved one makes towards positive change. Recognizing their commitment to personal growth reinforces their determination and encourages continued progress.

Seek Professional Guidance Together:

Consider seeking professional guidance together. Attending therapy sessions or counseling as a support system can enhance your understanding of HPD and provide tools for navigating challenges as a team.

Be Mindful of Your Well-being:

Prioritize your own well-being. Supporting someone with HPD can be challenging, and it's important to maintain your emotional and mental health. Seek your own support when needed and establish healthy boundaries to prevent burnout.

Express Unwavering Support:

Reiterate your unwavering support and commitment to the relationship. Let your loved one know that you are there for them through the ups and downs, fostering a sense of security and trust in the connection.

Remember that supporting someone with Histrionic Personality Disorder is a continuous journey, and your role as a supportive friend or family member is invaluable. By implementing these strategies, you contribute to a positive and growth-oriented environment for your loved one.

Professional Perspectives on Relationship Building with Histrionic Personality Disorder (HPD)

Understanding Individual Needs:

Professionals emphasize the importance of understanding the unique needs of individuals with HPD. Recognizing their desire for attention, validation, and intense emotional experiences allows for a more tailored approach to relationship building.

Building Trust Gradually:

Relationship building with someone with HPD often involves a gradual process of building trust. Professionals advocate for patience and consistency to establish a foundation of trust, creating a secure environment for the individual.

Clarifying Boundaries:

Clearly defining and communicating boundaries is crucial. Professionals stress the importance of expressing limits while maintaining empathy, helping individuals with HPD understand the parameters within which a healthy relationship can thrive.

Promoting Emotional Regulation:

Professionals focus on promoting emotional regulation techniques. Teaching individuals with HPD strategies to manage intense emotions contributes to more stable relationship dynamics and enhances their ability to navigate social interactions effectively.

Encouraging Self-Reflection:

Encouraging self-reflection is a key aspect of relationship building. Professionals guide individuals with HPD to explore their thoughts and emotions, fostering a deeper understanding of themselves and their impact on relationships.

Facilitating Effective Communication:

Professionals emphasize the need for effective communication skills. Both individuals and their partners benefit from learning and practicing communication techniques that promote understanding, active listening, and assertiveness.

Integrating Strengths-Based Approaches:

Incorporating strengths-based approaches is essential. Recognizing and building upon the strengths of individuals with HPD fosters a positive self-concept and contributes to the development of healthier relationship dynamics.

Navigating Attention-Seeking Behaviors:

Professionals guide partners and individuals to navigate attention-seeking behaviors with understanding. Addressing the underlying needs that drive these behaviors is crucial, creating opportunities for more meaningful connections.

Incorporating Cognitive-Behavioral Strategies:

Cognitive-behavioral strategies play a role in relationship building. Professionals utilize interventions that challenge negative thought patterns, promote adaptive behaviors, and contribute to more positive interpersonal interactions.

Collaborative Goal-Setting:

Collaborative goal-setting is encouraged. Professionals work with individuals and their partners to identify shared goals, aspirations, and milestones, fostering a sense of unity and purpose within the relationship.

Involving Support Systems:

Professionals highlight the importance of including support systems. Engaging with friends, family, or support groups provides additional resources for both individuals and their partners, creating a network that understands and supports the unique challenges of HPD.

Promoting Accountability:

Promoting accountability within the relationship is emphasized. Professionals guide individuals with HPD to take responsibility for their actions, fostering a sense of accountability that contributes to trust and stability.

Addressing Fear of Abandonment:

Addressing the fear of abandonment is a focal point. Professionals assist individuals with HPD in recognizing and managing this fear, helping them develop coping mechanisms and create more secure attachment patterns.

Integrating Mindfulness Practices:

Mindfulness practices are integrated into therapeutic approaches. Professionals encourage individuals with HPD to engage in mindfulness exercises, enhancing their self-awareness and emotional regulation skills within the context of relationships.

Promoting Relational Resilience:

Professionals work toward promoting relational resilience. Building resilience within the relationship involves equipping both individuals and their partners with the tools to navigate challenges, adapt to changes, and maintain a positive outlook.

Professional perspectives underscore the need for a comprehensive and empathetic approach to relationship building with Histrionic Personality Disorder. By integrating these strategies, individuals and their partners can cultivate healthier, more resilient connections that contribute to personal growth and well-being.

Couples Therapy as a Resource:

Couples therapy is often recommended as a valuable resource. Professionals stress the benefits of engaging in couples counseling, where both partners can openly address challenges, learn effective communication skills, and work collaboratively towards strengthening the relationship.

Empowering Partners through Education:

Professionals empower partners through education. Providing partners with information about Histrionic Personality Disorder, its traits, and effective coping strategies enhances their understanding, fostering empathy and informed support.

Fostering Positive Reinforcement:

Positive reinforcement is a powerful tool in relationship building. Professionals encourage partners to actively reinforce positive behaviors and achievements, creating a supportive environment that reinforces personal growth and mutual understanding.

Trauma-Informed Approaches:

Trauma-informed approaches are integrated into therapeutic interventions. Understanding the potential impact of past experiences on individuals with HPD guides professionals to adopt trauma-informed strategies that promote healing and resilience.

Integrating Attachment Theory:

Attachment theory is considered in understanding relationship dynamics. Professionals explore attachment patterns and work with individuals and their partners to cultivate more secure and adaptive attachment styles, addressing fears of abandonment and enhancing emotional security.

Teaching Conflict Resolution Skills:

Conflict resolution skills are taught to navigate relationship challenges. Professionals guide individuals and their partners in developing effective conflict resolution strategies, emphasizing compromise, active listening, and collaborative problem-solving.

Exploring Family Dynamics:

Exploring family dynamics contributes to a holistic understanding. Professionals consider family influences and dynamics, recognizing how past familial relationships may impact current interpersonal patterns. Addressing these dynamics fosters a comprehensive approach to relationship building.

Encouraging Individual and Joint Goals:

Professionals encourage the pursuit of both individual and joint goals. Collaboratively setting and achieving personal and relationship-oriented goals promotes a sense of accomplishment and reinforces the shared journey towards growth.

Utilizing Narrative Therapy Techniques:

Narrative therapy techniques are utilized to reshape narratives. Professionals help individuals with HPD and their partners reconstruct narratives, emphasizing strengths, resilience, and positive aspects of their shared story, fostering a more optimistic outlook.

Promoting a Growth Mindset:

Promoting a growth mindset is fundamental. Encouraging individuals and their partners to approach challenges with a growth mindset fosters adaptability, a willingness to learn, and an optimistic perspective on the potential for positive change.

Incorporating Expressive Therapies:

Expressive therapies, such as art or music therapy, are incorporated. These creative outlets provide individuals with alternative means of emotional expression and self-discovery, contributing to a more comprehensive therapeutic approach.

Validation of Experiences:

Validating experiences is central to therapeutic work. Professionals emphasize the importance of validating the experiences of both individuals and their partners, creating a space where emotions and perspectives are acknowledged without judgment.

Encouraging Peer Support:

Encouraging peer support is integral. Professionals recognize the value of individuals with HPD connecting with peers who share similar experiences. Peer support groups offer a sense of community, understanding, and shared coping strategies.

Highlighting Progress and Resilience:

Celebrating progress and resilience is a key aspect of therapy. Professionals consistently highlight achievements, no matter how small, fostering a sense of pride and reinforcing the resilience demonstrated by individuals and their partners.

Reinforcing Sustainable Relationship Practices:

Reinforcing sustainable relationship practices is a long-term goal. Professionals aim to equip individuals and their partners with tools and strategies that contribute to the sustainability of positive relationship practices, promoting lasting well-being.

Professional perspectives on relationship building with Histrionic Personality Disorder underscore the significance of a comprehensive, empathetic, and collaborative approach. By integrating these diverse strategies, professionals support individuals and their partners in navigating the complexities of HPD, fostering growth, and cultivating resilient relationships.

Chapter Five

Therapeutic Approaches and Interventions for Histrionic Personality Disorder (HPD)

Cognitive-Behavioral Therapy (CBT):

CBT is a foundational therapeutic approach. It helps individuals with HPD identify and challenge maladaptive thought patterns, develop healthier cognitive patterns, and acquire coping skills to manage intense emotions and behaviors.

Dialectical Behavior Therapy (DBT):

DBT combines cognitive-behavioral techniques with mindfulness strategies. It focuses on emotional regulation, interpersonal effectiveness, distress tolerance, and acceptance. DBT is particularly beneficial for individuals with HPD in enhancing emotional control and relational skills.

Psychodynamic Therapy:

Psychodynamic therapy explores unconscious thoughts and feelings that influence behavior. By delving into underlying psychological processes, individuals with HPD can gain insight into the origins of their behavior and work towards resolving deep-seated issues.

Mindfulness-Based Interventions:

Mindfulness techniques, such as meditation and mindful awareness, are integrated into therapeutic interventions. Mindfulness promotes self-awareness, emotional regulation, and a non-judgmental approach to experiences, addressing impulsive behaviors associated with HPD.

Schema Therapy:

Schema therapy focuses on identifying and restructuring maladaptive schemas, or core beliefs. Individuals with HPD can work with therapists to recognize and modify negative schemas, fostering healthier perceptions of themselves and their relationships.

Interpersonal Psychotherapy (IPT):

IPT targets interpersonal issues and focuses on improving communication and relational skills. For individuals with HPD, IPT helps enhance social functioning, navigate relationships more effectively, and address specific interpersonal challenges.

Expressive Therapies (Art, Music, Drama):

Expressive therapies provide alternative channels for emotional expression. Engaging in creative processes can help individuals with HPD explore and communicate their emotions in a non-verbal manner, contributing to self-discovery and emotional regulation.

Group Therapy:

Group therapy offers a supportive environment for individuals with HPD to interact with peers facing similar challenges. It provides opportunities for practicing interpersonal skills, receiving feedback, and building a sense of community.

Narrative Therapy:

Narrative therapy focuses on reauthoring personal narratives. Individuals with HPD can work with therapists to reconstruct their life stories, emphasizing strengths, resilience, and positive aspects, fostering a more adaptive self-concept.

Behavioral Interventions:

Behavioral interventions target specific behaviors associated with HPD. Therapists use reinforcement strategies to encourage positive behaviors and discourage maladaptive ones, promoting gradual change in behavioral patterns.

Family Therapy:

Family therapy involves the participation of family members to address relational dynamics. This approach helps improve communication, set boundaries, and educate family members about HPD, fostering a supportive environment for the individual.

Solution-Focused Brief Therapy (SFBT):

SFBT focuses on identifying solutions rather than dwelling on problems. Individuals with HPD work with therapists to set achievable goals and develop practical strategies for positive change, emphasizing strengths and resources.

Reality Therapy:

Reality therapy centers on addressing current behaviors and choices. Therapists help individuals with HPD take responsibility for their actions, make realistic plans for change, and focus on the present and future rather than dwelling on the past.

Integration of Pharmacotherapy:

In some cases, pharmacotherapy may be considered. Medications, such as antidepressants or mood stabilizers, may be prescribed to address co-occurring symptoms, such as depression or anxiety, under the guidance of a psychiatrist.

Continuum of Care Planning:

Therapeutic interventions often involve a continuum of care planning. This includes developing a long-term strategy for ongoing support, relapse prevention, and fostering sustained personal and relational growth.

Therapeutic approaches for Histrionic Personality Disorder are diverse, aiming to address the multifaceted aspects of the condition. Tailoring interventions to individual needs and preferences is key to promoting a collaborative therapeutic journey towards positive change.

Cognitive-Behavioral Techniques for Self-Reflection

Mindfulness Meditation:

Practice mindfulness meditation to bring attention to the present moment. By observing thoughts without judgment, individuals can enhance self-awareness, identify automatic cognitive patterns, and develop a more balanced perspective.

Daily Mood Tracking:

Keep a daily mood journal to track emotional patterns. Recording feelings and associated thoughts helps individuals recognize recurring cognitive themes, facilitating self-reflection on emotional responses to various situations.

ABC Model:

Utilize the ABC model (Activating event, Beliefs, Consequences) to analyze challenging situations. Identify the activating event, explore the beliefs or thoughts triggered, and assess the emotional and behavioral consequences. This framework enhances awareness of automatic thoughts.

Cognitive Restructuring:

Engage in cognitive restructuring by challenging negative thoughts. Identify irrational beliefs, evaluate evidence supporting or refuting them, and reframe thoughts in a more balanced and constructive manner. This technique promotes cognitive flexibility and resilience.

Behavioral Experiments:

Conduct behavioral experiments to test and challenge beliefs. Individuals can intentionally engage in activities that challenge their automatic thoughts, providing opportunities to gather new evidence and revise cognitive patterns through direct experience.

Socratic Questioning:

Employ Socratic questioning to explore the validity of thoughts. Ask yourself probing questions to examine the evidence, consider alternative perspectives, and identify cognitive distortions. This technique encourages more objective and reasoned self-analysis.

Cognitive Journaling:

Keep a cognitive journal to document recurring thought patterns. By regularly recording thoughts and associated emotions, individuals can identify trends, triggers, and cognitive biases, fostering self-awareness and insight into cognitive processes.

Identifying Cognitive Distortions:

Learn to recognize common cognitive distortions, such as all-or-nothing thinking, catastrophizing, or personalization. Identifying these distortions enhances self-reflection by pinpointing habitual patterns that may contribute to negative thought cycles.

Gratitude Practice:

Integrate a gratitude practice to shift focus toward positive aspects of life. Regularly acknowledging and recording moments of gratitude fosters a more optimistic mindset, promoting self-reflection on positive experiences and perspectives.

Cognitive ABCDE Technique:

Extend the ABC model with the D (Disputation) and E (New Effect) steps.

Dispute irrational beliefs by challenging them with evidence and developing more adaptive beliefs. Explore the new emotional and behavioral effects, reinforcing positive cognitive shifts.

Thought Records:

Use thought records to dissect and reframe specific situations. Record the situation, associated thoughts and emotions, cognitive distortions, and alternative, balanced thoughts. Thought records provide a structured approach to self-reflection in challenging scenarios.

Positive Self-Talk:

Cultivate positive self-talk by consciously replacing negative thoughts with affirming and constructive statements. This technique enhances self-compassion and fosters a more encouraging internal dialogue, contributing to a positive mindset.

Goal Setting and Monitoring:

Set realistic cognitive goals and monitor progress. Establish specific objectives related to changing cognitive patterns, track efforts to challenge and reframe thoughts, and celebrate achievements in developing healthier thought processes.

Visualization Techniques:

Use visualization techniques to imagine positive outcomes. Visualizing success and positive scenarios enhances optimism, reduces anxiety, and provides a platform for self-reflection on the potential for positive change.

Cognitive Flip Technique:

Implement the cognitive flip technique by transforming negative thoughts into positive affirmations. Identify negative self-talk and consciously flip it into a more empowering and constructive statement, fostering self-reflection and cultivating a positive mindset.

These cognitive-behavioral techniques empower individuals to engage in meaningful self-reflection, fostering awareness of thought patterns and promoting positive cognitive shifts. Regular practice enhances emotional well-being and contributes to the development of a more resilient and adaptive mindset.

Building a Supportive Network

Identify Trusted Individuals:

Identify individuals in your life whom you trust and feel comfortable confiding in. Trusted friends, family members, or colleagues can form the core of your supportive network.

Communicate Openly:

Foster open communication within your network. Share your thoughts, feelings, and concerns openly, allowing others to understand your experiences and offer support without judgment.

Educate Your Network:

Educate your network about Histrionic Personality Disorder (HPD). Providing information about the condition helps others better comprehend your challenges, foster empathy, and dispel misconceptions.

Set Clear Boundaries:

Establish clear boundaries within your relationships. Clearly communicate your needs and limitations, enabling your supportive network to respect and understand the parameters of your interactions.

Diversify Your Network:

Diversify your network to include a range of relationships. While close friends and family offer emotional support, consider involving mentors, support groups, or online communities to gain diverse perspectives and additional resources.

Join Support Groups:

Participate in support groups related to HPD. Connecting with individuals who share similar experiences provides a unique understanding and a supportive environment for discussing challenges and strategies.

Encourage Mutual Support:

Foster a culture of mutual support within your network. Encourage open dialogue where individuals can share their own challenges, creating an atmosphere of reciprocity and shared growth.

Express Your Needs:

Clearly express your needs to your supportive network. Whether you require emotional support, practical assistance, or simply someone to listen, communicating your needs helps others understand how best to support you.

Celebrate Achievements Together:

Celebrate achievements and milestones collectively. Sharing successes within your network reinforces positive experiences and contributes to a culture of encouragement and celebration.

Seek Professional Guidance Together:

If appropriate, involve your supportive network in aspects of your therapeutic journey. Attending therapy sessions together or discussing therapeutic strategies can enhance understanding and strengthen support systems.

Be Selective in Sharing:

Be selective when sharing personal information. While openness is important, it's equally crucial to share details selectively and appropriately based on the level of trust and comfort within each relationship.

Regular Check-Ins:

Establish a routine of regular check-ins. Regular communication ensures that your network remains aware of your well-being, allowing them to provide support when needed and fostering a consistent connection.

Utilize Technology:

Leverage technology to stay connected. Virtual platforms, messaging apps, or social media can facilitate ongoing communication, making it easier to maintain connections even in busy or physically distant circumstances.

Practice Active Listening:

Cultivate active listening skills within your network. Encourage members to listen empathetically, ask clarifying questions, and validate each other's experiences, creating a supportive and understanding environment.

Acknowledge and Express Gratitude:

Acknowledge the support you receive and express gratitude. Regularly expressing appreciation reinforces the value of your network, fostering a positive and reciprocal dynamic.

Building a supportive network involves intentional efforts to nurture connections and create an environment of understanding and empathy. By incorporating these strategies, you can cultivate a network that contributes to your well-being and growth.

Cultivating Resilience and Shaping a Positive Future Outlook

Develop a Growth Mindset:

Cultivate a growth mindset by viewing challenges as opportunities for learning and personal development. Embrace the belief that abilities and intelligence can be developed over time, fostering resilience in the face of adversity.

Set Realistic Goals:

Set realistic and achievable goals. Break larger objectives into smaller, manageable steps, allowing for a sense of accomplishment along the way. Realistic goals contribute to a positive outlook by acknowledging progress.

Embrace Self-Compassion:

Practice self-compassion by treating yourself with kindness and understanding. Embracing self-compassion during difficult moments fosters resilience and helps you navigate challenges with greater emotional well-being.

Foster Social Connections:

Prioritize social connections and cultivate meaningful relationships. Building a supportive network provides emotional sustenance and reinforces a positive outlook by offering shared experiences and understanding.

Learn from Setbacks:

View setbacks as opportunities for growth. Analyze challenges, extract lessons, and apply newfound knowledge to future situations. Learning from setbacks contributes to resilience and shapes a forward-focused perspective.

Build Emotional Regulation Skills

Develop emotional regulation skills to navigate intense emotions effectively. Techniques such as mindfulness, deep breathing, and self-reflection contribute to emotional resilience and a more balanced outlook.

Celebrate Small Wins:

Celebrate small victories and achievements. Acknowledging and celebrating incremental successes boosts confidence, reinforces positive behavior, and contributes to an optimistic future outlook.

Cultivate Flexibility:

Cultivate flexibility in adapting to change. Resilience is strengthened when individuals can adjust to new circumstances, embrace uncertainty, and approach challenges with adaptability and a willingness to learn.

Practice Mindfulness Meditation:

Incorporate mindfulness meditation into your routine. Mindfulness fosters present-moment awareness, reduces stress, and enhances resilience by promoting a calm and centered approach to life's challenges.

Engage in Reflective Practices:

Engage in reflective practices, such as journaling or self-reflection exercises. Regularly reviewing experiences, emotions, and personal growth fosters self-awareness and contributes to a positive narrative about the future.

Seek Professional Support:

If needed, seek professional support to navigate the challenges. Therapy or counseling can provide valuable tools, insights, and strategies to build resilience and shape a positive outlook on the future.

Nurture Physical Well-Being:

Prioritize physical well-being through regular exercise, balanced nutrition, and sufficient rest. Physical health contributes to mental and emotional resilience, creating a foundation for a positive future outlook.

Develop Coping Strategies:

Identify and develop effective coping strategies for managing stress and adversity. Having a repertoire of coping mechanisms enhances resilience and equips you to face future challenges with greater confidence.

Focus on Solutions:

Shift focus from problems to solutions. Adopt a problem-solving mindset that actively seeks constructive solutions. Addressing challenges proactively contributes to a sense of control and optimism about the future.

Engage in Meaningful Activities:

Engage in activities that bring a sense of purpose and fulfillment. Pursuing meaningful interests and goals fosters a positive future outlook by creating a sense of direction and personal satisfaction.

Cultivating resilience involves intentional practices and a mindset that embraces growth and adaptation. By incorporating these strategies, you can shape a positive future outlook and navigate life's challenges with resilience and optimism.

Printed in Great Britain
by Amazon